This We Believe

Keys to Educating Young Adolescents

The position paper of the Association for Middle Level Education

Association for Middle Level Education
Westerville, Ohio

Association for Middle Level Education

4151 Executive Parkway, Suite 300, Westerville, Ohio 43081
tel: 800.528.6672   fax: 614.895.4750   www.amle.org

Cover Photo: Thank you to the staff and students of Blendon Middle School and Christina McDonald. Photo by Alan Geho.

ISBN: 978-156090-232-4

From the Executive Director

This We Believe: Keys to Educating Young Adolescents is the foundational document of the Association for Middle Level Education (AMLE), formerly National Middle School Association. The document identifies the essential characteristics of middle grades schools and the characteristics of young adolescents, students ages 10 to 15. This fourth edition of the association's position paper, authorized by the Board of Trustees, applies updated research to the 16 characteristics and four essential attributes of successful middle grades schools.

The association's members and Board of Trustees approved a name change for the association in spring 2011. However, the name change did not change the association's mission, which remains

> *The Association for Middle Level Education is dedicated to improving the educational experiences of young adolescents by providing vision, knowledge, and resources to all who serve them in order to develop healthy, productive, and ethical citizens.*

The development of this landmark document engaged hundreds of dedicated educators with a singular focus—to do what's best for kids. We are indebted to the contributors, writers, and reviewers who aided in the development of this edition of *This We Believe*. This living document is designed to improve middle grades practices by focusing on the importance of understanding the nature of this age group. This is, indeed, the key to helping all young adolescents succeed.

William D. Waidelich, Ed.D.
Executive Director

Contents

Contents continued

Introduction

The Association for Middle Level Education (AMLE), formerly National Middle School Association, believes that educational programs for young adolescents should reflect what research and vast experience have demonstrated to be best for 10- to 15-year-olds. Based on that belief, the association has set forth in this document the tenets that will provide sound guidance for those responsible for designing programs committed to improving both learning and learners.

Its release comes at a time when research, practice, and common sense tell us that middle level education is the crucial link in the pre-K–16 continuum. During these transitional years, students change significantly—physically, intellectually, morally, psychologically, and social-emotionally. The academic growth and personal development experienced during these important years significantly impact their futures. In the middle grades, the stage will be set for success in high school and beyond, or for disengagement and the likelihood of becoming a high school dropout.

Given the key role middle level education plays in ensuring every young adolescent becomes a healthy, productive, and ethical adult, it is critical that this document be read carefully, reflected on and understood fully, and then used by all who are concerned about the education of young adolescents.

Several terms involving the word middle are used throughout this document. What began as the middle school movement in the 1960s was an extension of the reorganization of secondary education that was launched in the early

1900s. In the 1980s, the term middle level education came into use and puts the focus on the level of education that serves young adolescents rather than on a school organization or grade plan. In this document, middle level education is used when the reference is to the larger effort. Middle grades, a more recently employed term, is used when the teachers or specific practices in those grades is the focus.

The Importance of
Middle Level Education

Every day, millions of diverse, rapidly changing 10- to 15-year-olds make critical and complex life choices and form the attitudes, values, and dispositions that will direct their behavior as adults. They deserve an education that will enhance their healthy growth as lifelong learners, ethical and democratic citizens, and increasingly competent, self-sufficient individuals who are optimistic about the future and prepared to succeed in our ever-changing world.

It is important to recall and understand the beginnings of the middle school movement. In 1963, Dr. William Alexander, a noted curriculum authority, spoke at a Cornell University conference convened to examine the status and future of the junior high school. In his presentation entitled "The Junior High School: A Changing View," he focused on curriculum and instruction, providing participants with a thoughtful and challenging proposal to implement a new "middle school" taught by specifically prepared educators who would implement a relevant curriculum and essential learning processes that were developmentally appropriate for students within this age range.

In describing his vision, Alexander quoted an educational belief statement of the Winnetka (Illinois) Public Schools where he had been superintendent:

>*...Intellectual growth means much more than an increasing competence*
>*in the academic content of the curriculum. We must endeavor to*

stimulate in the child a love for learning, an attitude of inquiry, a passion for truth and beauty, a questioning mind. The learning of right answers is not enough . . . beyond answers alone, we must help children ask the right questions, and discover their answers through creative thinking, reasoning, judging, and understanding.

Alexander's proposed framework resonated not only with the conference's participants but also with others who were focused on educating 10- to 15-year-olds. A call for action went forth, and the middle school movement began.

His belief that "the learning of right answers is not enough," is even more relevant today than it was in 1963. Continuing research and practice since Alexander's initial call for a "middle school" have shown the importance of implementing schools that openly address both the academic and personal development of every young adolescent.

Contemporary society has remarkably different challenges from those that educators faced just a decade or two ago. While the traditional school functions—conveying fundamental knowledge, teaching the tools of communication and scholarship, and promoting democratic citizenship—remain valid, achieving these functions while meeting academic imperatives and other new responsibilities requires relevant curriculum and engaging teaching strategies that will empower each student to be successful in a global society. Thriving now and in the future requires becoming a lifelong learner and demands more than a basic understanding of reading, writing, and mathematics. It requires the ability to apply sophisticated skills in a variety of settings and solve complex problems individually and in collaboration with others.

> Thriving now and in the future requires becoming a lifelong learner and demands more than a basic understanding of reading, writing, and mathematics.

The curriculum, pedagogy, and programs of middle grades schools must be based upon the developmental readiness, needs, and interests of young adolescents. This concept is at the heart of middle level education. The Association for Middle Level Education's (AMLE's) advocacy is based exclusively on what research and experience have shown to be best for young adolescents.

When developing and sustaining successful middle grades schools, educators and others involved must consider the intent of the various concepts, specific programs, or operational features recommended. They should ask, "What is the ultimate purpose of this program?" "What are we trying to accomplish?" or "How will it affect student growth, development, and achievement?"

Perhaps the most profound and enduring lesson learned in more than 40 years of active middle school practice, research, and advocacy is that the attributes and characteristics recommended in *This We Believe: Keys to Educating Young Adolescents* are interdependent and should be implemented in concert. In the early years of the middle school movement, educators often selectively adopted those characteristics that appeared to be achievable or more appropriate for a school or particular situation. These characteristics are parts of a larger whole; successful schools for young adolescents must implement the full range of structures, supports, and practices known to be most effective with this age group. It is vitally important to recognize that the areas of development—physical, intellectual, moral, psychological, and social-emotional—are inexorably intertwined, making the achievement of academic success highly dependent upon the other developmental needs also being met.

Young adolescents

Young people undergo more rapid and profound personal changes between the ages 10 and 15 than at any other time in their lives. Although growth in infancy is also very extensive, infants are not the conscious witnesses of their own development. Early adolescence is also a period of tremendous variability among youngsters of the same gender and chronological age in all areas of their development. Changes occur irregularly, as young adolescents enter puberty at different times and progress at different rates. Individual differences proliferate, making dubious such assumptions as, "All seventh graders are . . . ." Socioeconomic status, privilege, and ethnicity are among factors that add to the diversity of students.

Changes in the patterns of thinking become evident in the ideas and questions middle grades students express about the world and how it functions. These shifts may be apparent in the questions they pose to each other and to trusted adults, in their reflections about personal experiences, in their views on moral issues, and through their perceptions of stories, images, and humor. They reveal new capacities for thinking about how they learn, for considering multiple ideas, and for planning steps to carry out their own learning activities. However, because cognitive growth occurs gradually and sporadically, most middle grades students still require ongoing, concrete, experiential learning in order to achieve.

Early adolescence is characterized by accelerated yet uneven movement toward reproductive maturity. Hormonal shifts trigger physical transformations such as redistribution of body fat, increases in weight and height, abrupt bone and muscle growth, and changes in voice, hair, and complexion. In general, physical maturation begins considerably earlier for girls than boys. Sexual development prompts new physical, emotional, and social concerns for both sexes. Early or late physical maturation affects self-perception as well as status with peers and adults.

Concerns about appearance and body image usually generate heightened interest in personal grooming among young adolescents. Yet, their health choices are often inappropriate, such as when they select foods inadequate for meeting the nutritional needs of their changing bodies. In addition, some youngsters begin experimenting with tobacco, alcohol, harmful drugs, and sex, all of which pose serious, potential threats to personal health. Rapid physical changes combined with the multiple hazards of contemporary life make early adolescence a crucial period for developing healthy personal habits.

Typically, parents or guardians retain primary authority and continue as the source of basic values for children. However, young people's desire for peer acceptance and the need to belong to particular social groups are often intense and sometimes lead to shifting allegiance from adults to peers. Other young adolescents, the environment, and the media increasingly influence issues of right and wrong, good and bad, and appropriate and inappropriate behavior. Family members should recognize the reticence of young adolescents to communicate with family members as part of their striving for independence. Family members, however, should take care to keep their end of the communication line open. Caregivers and educators must remember that young adolescents hunger for informal interactions and conversations with caring adults.

Rapid physical changes make early adolescence a crucial period for developing healthy personal habits.

The decisions young people make are difficult in a world where violence and the exploitation of vulnerable youth are all too prevalent. Young people receive conflicting messages about sexuality and appropriate behavior; often their schools and even parents may shy away from discussing such issues with them. Educators in developmentally responsive middle grades schools construct curricula that not only provide clear, complete, and objective information, but actively assist young people in formulating positive moral principles. This guidance, of course, must reflect sensitivity and consider family, cultural, and community expectations.

The several developmental processes associated with adolescence, while natural and necessary, present challenges to those entrusted with the responsibility for the healthy development and education of young adolescents. It is very clear that yesterday's schools are ill suited for meeting the challenges young adolescents face today.

The changing world

The many transitions individuals undergo during early adolescence would make growing up difficult enough in an unchanging world. Today, however, changes abound in every aspect of society. The influences of electronic and print media, the increasingly diverse and multicultural nature of communities, and a growing international influence impact education. Family makeup is also more varied—by gender, race, religion, or ethnicity of parents or guardians. Although modern life is richer in many ways, the roles and benchmarks for youth have become increasingly ambiguous. Too many children lack adequate supervision in their out-of-school hours. Without responsible adult role models unhealthy situations exist when young adolescents live in an environment rife with temptations.

Although physical maturity occurs earlier than in previous generations, today's children still confront the same developmental hurdles. During early adolescence they need information that helps them understand the physical and other changes in their lives. They also need supportive adult guidance and advocacy more than ever as they struggle to maintain the hope and optimism that have characterized youth.

Schools have a responsibility to assist students in dealing with major societal issues.

That hope and optimism is often further threatened by socioeconomic pressures and misinformation directed at young adolescents. Many students around the world have disposable income and are targets of marketing campaigns that are by definition manipulative. Such marketing is frequently linked to attractive entertainment options available to young adolescents—options that often foster superficial and selfish values, depict gender roles inappropriately, and promote a passive, consumer-oriented, and at times, self-destructive lifestyle. Given the global pervasiveness of the media, students everywhere who have little or no money live exposed to the same marketing and social pressures, yet face added feelings of frustration and helplessness due to their lack of resources.

Young adolescents also witness and experience the negative results of homelessness, racism, drug and alcohol abuse, crime, international terrorism, wars, domestic violence, and child abuse. Schools that serve them have a responsibility to assist students in dealing with such major societal issues. Schools and community programs foster responsible, moral decision makers and discriminating, enlightened consumers.

The guidelines that teachers and administrators follow in selecting educational goals, curriculum content, and instructional and assessment processes grow out of an awareness of and respect for the nature of these distinctive young adolescents. Educators who understand these young people and the cultural context in which they grow to maturity will make informed decisions about the kinds of schools and learning experiences that young adolescents need.

Major Goals of Middle Level Education

~~~oooooooooooooooooooooooooooooooooooooooooooooooooooooo~~~

Each young adolescent is a living work in progress with growth along the road to maturity occurring at different times and rates. As a result, designing middle grades programs on the assumption that every student is ready to master specific concepts or content at precisely the same time is unrealistic and counterproductive.

We can, however, design programs that offer abundant and meaningful opportunities for each young adolescent to grow and develop an appetite for learning and acquire needed skills and knowledge.

The Association for Middle Level Education asserts that in order to become a fully functioning, self-actualized person, each young adolescent should

» Become actively aware of the larger world, asking significant and relevant questions about that world and wrestling with big ideas and questions for which there may not be one right answer.

» Be able to think rationally and critically and express thoughts clearly.

» Read deeply to independently gather, assess, and interpret information from a variety of sources and read avidly for enjoyment and lifelong learning.

» Use digital tools to explore, communicate, and collaborate with the world and learn from the rich and varied resources available.

» Be a good steward of the earth and its resources and a wise and intelligent consumer of the wide array of goods and services available.

» Understand and use the major concepts, skills, and tools of inquiry in the areas of health and physical education, language arts, world languages, mathematics, natural and physical sciences, and the social sciences.

» Explore music, art, and careers, and recognize their importance to personal growth and learning.

» Develop his or her strengths, particular skills, talents, or interests and have an emerging understanding of his or her potential contributions to society and to personal fulfillment.

» Recognize, articulate, and make responsible, ethical decisions concerning his or her own health and wellness needs.

» Respect and value the diverse ways people look, speak, think, and act within the immediate community and around the world.

» Develop the interpersonal and social skills needed to learn, work, and play with others harmoniously and confidently.

» Assume responsibility for his or her own actions and be cognizant of and ready to accept obligations for the welfare of others.

» Understand local, national, and global civic responsibilities and demonstrate active citizenship through participation in endeavors that serve and benefit those larger communities.

Essential Attributes
and Characteristics

To guide and support students in their quest to achieve these goals, AMLE further affirms that an education for young adolescents must be

1. **Developmentally responsive:** using the distinctive nature of young adolescents as the foundation upon which all decisions about school organization, policies, curriculum, instruction, and assessment are made.

2. **Challenging:** ensuring that every student learns and every member of the learning community is held to high expectations.

3. **Empowering:** providing all students with the knowledge and skills they need to take responsibility for their lives, to address life's challenges, to function successfully at all levels of society, and to be creators of knowledge.

4. **Equitable:** advocating for and ensuring every student's right to learn and providing appropriately challenging and relevant learning opportunities for every student.

AMLE believes that these four essential attributes of successful middle level education can be realized and achieved best through the 16 characteristics displayed in the following chart and detailed individually in subsequent sections. To understand them better, these characteristics are grouped in three categories—Curriculum, Instruction, and Assessment; Leadership and Organization; Culture and Community. The characteristics are, however, interdependent and need to be implemented in concert.

16 Characteristics

Curriculum, Instruction, and Assessment

Educators value young adolescents and are prepared to teach them. *Value Young Adolescents*

Students and teachers are engaged in active, purposeful learning. *Active Learning*

Curriculum is challenging, exploratory, integrative, and relevant. *Challenging Curriculum*

Educators use multiple learning and teaching approaches. *Multiple Learning Approaches*

Varied and ongoing assessments advance learning as well as measure it. *Varied Assessments*

Leadership and Organization

A shared vision developed by all stakeholders guides every decision. *Shared Vision*

Leaders are committed to and knowledgeable about this age group, educational research, and best practices. *Committed Leaders*

Leaders demonstrate courage and collaboration. *Courageous & Collaborative Leaders*

Ongoing professional development reflects best educational practices. *Professional Development*

Organizational structures foster purposeful learning and meaningful relationships. *Organizational Structures*

Culture and Community

The school environment is inviting, safe, inclusive, and supportive of all. *School Environment*

Every student's academic and personal development is guided by an adult advocate. *Adult Advocate*

Comprehensive guidance and support services meet the needs of young adolescents. *Guidance Services*

Health and wellness are supported in curricula, school-wide programs, and related policies. *Health & Wellness*

The school actively involves families in the education of their children. *Family Involvement*

Essential Attributes

An education for young adolescents must be

Developmentally Responsive
using the nature of young adolescents as the foundation on which all decisions are made.

Challenging
recognizing that every student can learn and everyone is held to high expectations.

Empowering
providing all students with the knowledge and skills they need to take control of their lives.

Equitable
advocating for every student's right to learn and providing challenging and relevant learning opportunities.

The Association for Middle Level Education

Successful Schools
for
Young Adolescents

Curriculum, Instruction, and Assessment Characteristics

Educators value young adolescents and are prepared to teach them. (Value Young Adolescents)

Effective middle grades teachers and administrators choose to work with and advocate for young adolescents. Through specific middle grades professional preparation prior to teaching young adolescents and continuous professional development as they pursue their careers, they understand the developmental uniqueness of this age group, the appropriate curriculum, and effective learning and assessment strategies. Such educators are collaborators who know how to form learning partnerships with their students, demonstrating empathy while engaging them in significant academic learning experiences.

Middle grades educators enjoy being with young adolescents, and understand the dynamics of the ever-changing youth culture. These educators value interdisciplinary studies and integrative learning and make sound pedagogical, research-based decisions reflecting the needs, interests, and special abilities of students. They are sensitive to individual differences and varied learning styles, respond positively to the many dimensions of diversity students present, and are effective in involving families in the education of their children.

Such educators are inevitably role models for students. They realize their own behavior sends influential messages to young adolescents and so practice those qualities of heart and mind they want young adolescents to emulate. They model inclusive, democratic, and team-oriented approaches to teaching and learning. They provide leadership in ongoing efforts to improve the school's effectiveness. When such dedicated and knowledgeable middle grades educators work together, they create exciting learning experiences for all students; their professional commitment and passion make a positive difference in the life of every young adolescent they teach.

State departments of education, professional practice boards, and institutions of higher learning share responsibility for developing appropriate programs to provide both initial preparation and graduate programs leading to specific middle grades teacher and administrator preparation and middle grades licensure. Although schools and school districts have a prime responsibility for providing ongoing professional development, they should also use the resources that are provided by state departments, colleges, universities, and professional associations.

Students and teachers are engaged in active, purposeful learning. (Active Learning)

Successful middle grades schools are characterized by the active engagement of students and teachers. It could not be otherwise, for everything that is known about the nature of young adolescents and the principles of learning points to the reality that the most successful learning strategies are ones that involve each student personally. As they develop the ability to hypothesize, organize information into useful and meaningful constructs, and grasp long-term cause and effect relationships, students demonstrate they are ready for and should play a major role in their own education. Successful middle grades practices purposefully empower young adolescents to assume this role, one that includes self-advocacy. Through planned opportunities for students to express their needs and preferences, middle grades educators open new pathways to facilitate differentiated instruction and authentic assessment. These, in turn, enhance and accelerate learning.

> The most successful learning strategies are ones that involve each student personally.

Developmentally responsive middle grades educators take the concept of hands-on activities further by promoting what might be termed "hands-joined" activities, ones that teachers and students work together in developing. Such activities foster student ownership and lead to levels of understanding unlikely to be achieved when students are simply completing teacher-made assignments. Additionally, learning experiences are greatly enhanced when all students have the technology to access rich content, communicate with others, write for authentic audiences, and collaborate with other learners next door or across the globe.

When students routinely assume the role of teacher, and teachers demonstrate that they are still learners, the conditions of a genuine learning community are present. Teachers participate actively in learning activities rather than just being observers of students at work. Such collaboration leads to increased achievement, demonstrates democratic processes, and furthers meaningful student-teacher relationships.

Curriculum is challenging, exploratory, integrative, and relevant. (Challenging Curriculum)

Curriculum is the primary vehicle for achieving the goals and objectives of a school. In developmentally responsive middle grades schools, curriculum encompasses every planned aspect of the educational program. It includes not only the basic classes designed to advance skills and knowledge but also school-wide services and programs such as guidance, clubs and interest groups, music and drama productions, student government, service activities, and sports.

Recognizing that covering the content and learning the content are not synonymous, and that having valuable academic standards neither implies nor demands a uniform, prescribed curriculum, middle grades teachers and curriculum developers must work diligently to provide appropriate educational experiences for young adolescents. An effective middle grades curriculum is distinguished by learning experiences that address societal expectations while appealing to young adolescents and offering them opportunities to pose and answer questions that are important to them. In other words, an effective middle grades curriculum must be challenging, exploratory, integrative, and relevant, from both the student's and the teacher's perspective.

In some exemplary middle level schools, curriculum is often carried out in units or projects that involve complex tasks and focus on major issues. Units are organized around a theme or integrated by a melding of teachers' goals and students' questions rather than through separate subjects.

The "hidden curriculum"—what students learn indirectly but surely from the people with whom they interact, the structures in which they work, and the issues that inevitably occur in a human enterprise—has a powerful influence on students' education. In fact, this aspect of learning is sometimes so profound and long lasting that it overrides learning that is more traditional. Lives are often shaped more by small individual actions, probing questions, subtle reminders, earned commendations, and personalized challenges than by direct instruction. Young lives are too often strained by subtle restrictions implicit within the curriculum structures and school strategies. Teachers in successful middle grades schools skillfully interweave the planned curriculum with the unplanned, ensuring that interactions with students are positive and that each student is valued and treated equitably.

Challenging

Marshalling their sustained interests and efforts, challenging curriculum actively engages young adolescents. It addresses substantive issues and skills, is geared to their levels of understanding, and increasingly enables them to assume control of their own learning.

Learning tasks must be perceived as achievable, even if difficult, reflecting the high expectations held for all. Having students grapple with and master advanced concepts and skills requires middle grades teachers to stretch themselves, moving well beyond "covering material." Using their professional judgment and in consultation with students, they guide the selection of ideas for in-depth study from that vast range of information and materials that are genuinely important and worth knowing. For these issues to come alive, teachers must help students examine values, assumptions, basic principles, and alternative points of view, addressing why things happen as well as how. Skills and concepts are mastered in context as students are helped to become explorers, thinkers, and skilled writers. Such an approach becomes all the more critical as technology makes the what, when, who, and even the how aspects of knowledge universally and readily accessible. With overwhelming amounts of data instantly available, true learning places emphasis on the understanding of basic concepts and on the ability to use information in forming creative solutions.

Given the developmental diversity present in every middle grades classroom, gearing curriculum to each student's level of understanding is a complex task. In addition to varied learning styles and different rates of development, young adolescents' cultural backgrounds and prior experiences must be taken into account along with the impact of inclusion. Adapting curriculum to challenge and provide continuous progress for each and every student requires significant planning, flexibility, and collaboration among all teachers, counselors, school social workers, parents, and the students themselves.

Both content and methods must be diversified and individualized. As a first step, teachers can offer choices among learning activities, providing challenges for every student to reach and grow according to each individual's abilities and readiness. Independent study, small group work, special interest enrichment experiences, and apprenticeships are among means of addressing individual needs.

Having students grapple with and master advanced concepts and skills requires teachers to stretch themselves, moving well beyond "covering material."

Because of young adolescents' drive toward independence, they should be provided with opportunities to contribute to and take ownership of their own educations. Consonant with their varying capacities to handle responsibility, students must be nurtured in making choices and decisions about curricular goals, content, and activities, as well as the means of assessment. Initiative, responsibility, leadership, and an understanding of the democratic way of life are fostered by opportunities to participate in team governance and in various aspects of school life.

Exploratory

The middle school is the finding place; for young adolescents, by nature, are adventuresome, curious explorers. Therefore, the general approach for the entire curriculum at this level should be exploratory. Exploration, in fact, is the aspect of a successful middle school curriculum that most directly and fully reflects the nature and needs of the majority of young adolescents, most of whom are ready for an exploratory process. Although some experiences or courses may be labeled exploratory, it should not be assumed they are, therefore, nonacademic. The reverse is equally true; a solid academic experience properly designed is exploratory. Exploration is an attitude and approach, not a classification of content.

As students come of age, the exploratory responsibility of the middle level is particularly critical. In many respects, this level of school often presents a last chance. If youth pass through early adolescence without broad, exploratory experiences, their future lives may be needlessly restricted. They deserve opportunities to ascertain their special interests and aptitudes, to engage in activities that will broaden their views of the world and of themselves. They need, for instance, the chance to conduct science experiments, though they may never work in a lab, to be a member of a musical group, though never to become a professional musician, to write in multiple formats, though never to publish professionally, to have a part in a play, though never to become a paid actor, to play on a team, though never to become a career athlete, or to create visual images through drawing and painting, though never to become an artist.

> Exploration is an attitude and approach, not a classification of content.

Curriculum that is exploratory has potential career value and also leads to healthy recreational and leisure time pursuits that enrich life and help develop well-rounded, self-sufficient adults. Exploratory and enrichment experiences are fundamental components of a school serving young adolescents and deserve their rightful place in the curriculum and the schedule. Advances in technology give exploration a whole new dimension, and schools must provide regular access to digital tools for every student.

Integrative

Effective middle grades schools provide experiences, studies, and units, directed either by individual teachers or preferably by teams, that are specifically designed to be integrative; for that is how learning is maximized. Reading, writing, speaking, and listening should be advanced and practiced wherever they apply, rather than taught in isolation. Moreover, all teachers should help students see how content and skills learned in school are applicable in their daily lives.

Curriculum is integrative when it helps students make sense of their lives and the world around them, and when students are empowered to share in making significant, meaningful decisions about their learning. An integrative curriculum revolves around important questions students ask, rather than around a predetermined body of content. Such curriculum is coherent when knowledge and skills deemed crucial by the adult community, as expressed in academic standards, are applied to student concerns. Since real-life issues raised by students are by nature multifaceted, attention to them integrates the curriculum in natural ways.

Furthermore, student-generated questions lead to demanding study. Whereas prescribed curricula often focus on finding answers to questions young adolescents never ask, critical thinking, decision making, and creativity are enhanced when students examine problems they have identified and take steps to solve them. In such cases, they produce or construct knowledge rather than simply being consumers of information given. An integrative curriculum also provides students opportunities to reflect on their experiences and to articulate their progress, essential steps toward recognizing and accepting responsibility for their own learning.

Relevant

Curriculum is relevant when it allows students to pursue answers to questions they have about themselves, the content, and the world. When teachers help them see the many connections that link various topics and subjects, students recognize the holistic nature of all knowledge. They need to study concepts and learn skills in areas that interest them as well as in those determined by adults.

Almost any aspect of a school's curriculum may be relevant to a young adolescent when developed with reference to that student's questions, ideas, and concerns. Students further relate these questions and content to issues within their schools or broader community through service-learning activities that research identifies as enhancing academic success. Making curriculum relevant, however, does not mean that topics and material to be studied should be limited to students' preexisting interests. Relevant curriculum creates new interests, opening doors to new knowledge and opportunities for "stretching" students to higher levels of learning. This includes introducing students to concepts and skills that have become particularly important to successful living in the 21st century, with its global perspectives and requirements for facility with digital tools.

Educators use multiple learning and teaching approaches. (Multiple Learning Approaches)

The distinctive developmental characteristics of young adolescents provide the foundation for selecting learning and teaching strategies, just as they do for designing curriculum. Teaching approaches should capitalize on the skills, abilities, and prior knowledge of young adolescents; use multiple intelligences; involve students' individual learning styles; and recognize the need for regular physical movement. Students should acquire various ways of posing and answering questions and engage in learning situations wherein basic skills are mastered in functional contexts. When learning experiences capitalize on students' cultural, experiential, and personal backgrounds, new concepts build on knowledge students already possess.

Since young adolescents learn best through engagement and interaction, learning strategies should involve students in dialogue with teachers and with one another about what to study and how best to study topics selected. While some direct, teacher-centered instruction is in order, varied approaches are needed including experiments, demonstrations, surveys and opinion polls, simulations, inquiry-based and group projects, community-based services, and independent study. Individual differences are accommodated through abundant opportunities for student choice within classes and in co-curricular programs. Experiences are provided that appeal to students' special talents or interests, whether they are intellectual, athletic, or artistic.

> All educators must become proficient in using technology and integrating it throughout the curriculum.

Teachers of various specialties collaborate and cooperate to design learning activities that ensure appropriate challenges for all students. Varying forms of group work are used to increase student engagement and achievement, with students being clustered for short periods of time randomly, or by ability, interest, or other criteria. School personnel involve the families of students in determining the best educational program.

Instructional materials and resources are most worthwhile when they provide multiple viewpoints and encourage young adolescents to explore new ideas. Educators provide students with supplementary print and non-print resources related to topics being investigated. The community is a major educational resource, providing varied learning experiences and resource persons for ongoing classroom studies. The research possibilities for students using the Internet are unlimited, allowing for global connections that will provide varied perspectives, insights, and contacts not available in a single school or community.

Through preservice preparation programs and ongoing professional development, all educators must become proficient in using technology and integrating it throughout the curriculum. Not ends in themselves, digital tools open up new instructional and learning opportunities that develop higher-order thinking skills and provide the most current information. Such tools enable teachers and students to interact with real-world resources in unprecedented ways, communicating with other students, teachers, and experts around the world. Properly used and widely available, digital tools not only accelerate and simplify many routine tasks but potentially change the very nature of instruction, democratizing both content and the learning process. Understanding and using digital tools help students develop personal responsibility and independence and prepare them for contemporary life. Finally, students need to investigate the many ramifications of what it means to live in a technological society and become fully informed and wise consumers of modern media.

Varied and ongoing assessments advance learning as well as measure it. (Varied Assessments)

Continuous, authentic, and appropriate assessment measures provide evidence about each student's learning progress. Such information helps students, teachers, and family members select immediate learning goals and plan further education.

Although the words are often used interchangeably, assessment and evaluation are distinctly different functions. Assessment is the process of describing a student's progress toward an objective. Evaluation, also called summative assessment, uses data to place a value or judgment on actions or products. Evaluation can also be used to determine the effectiveness of a program, leading to its improvement. Assessment, which does advance and guide learning, should include both the processes and the products of learning, taking into account student differences.

Students should have opportunities to set personal goals, chart their growth, and reflect on their progress in achieving the knowledge, skills, and behavioral objectives of education. Means of assessing student progress should also serve a learning function, helping students to clarify their understandings and providing information on which to base judgments. Grades alone are inadequate for reporting student progress, particularly using grades in the formative assessment phase, when they inhibit students' learning.

> Means of assessing student progress should serve a learning function, helping students clarify understandings and providing information on which to base judgments.

Each classroom should have a balance between formative assessment for the advancement of learning and summative assessment for the evaluation of learning. Both have roles to play but serve distinctly different purposes; both should provide students with opportunities to demonstrate their learning in a variety of ways.

Teachers should specify in advance the criteria for assessment, usually in the form of a rubric that defines levels of quality for assessing performance, demonstrations, projects, or similar work; and examples of quality work should be readily available. Because young adolescents are capable of being active participants in both assessing and judging their accomplishments, they should be involved in designing these rubrics. This promotes students' having an integral understanding of the work and internalizing levels of quality, expressed in terminology that is understandable and defining.

In addition to the content knowledge and skills typically assessed through paper and pencil tests, methods of assessing students' growth must address the many other aspects of a student's development including critical thinking, independence, responsibility, and those other desired personal attributes and dispositions that have lifelong influence. This requires a variety of assessment strategies including journals, electronic portfolios, demonstrations, descriptive teacher feedback, peer feedback, teacher-designed tests, and audio or video evidences of learning. The use of formative assessment is critical in keeping students on the path to academic success.

In developmentally responsive middle level schools, assessment procedures also reflect the unique characteristics of young adolescents. Assessment should emphasize individual progress rather than comparison with other students and should not rely on extrinsic motivation. The goal is to help students discover and understand their own strengths, weaknesses, interests, and aptitudes. Student self-assessment helps develop a fair and realistic self-concept. Young adolescents' concern with peer approval is another reason to emphasize individualized assessment rather than comparisons with others.

Educators should recognize students' efforts and support their developing work ethic, knowing that not all students can reach a uniform standard at the same time. Emphasis should be on what has been accomplished. Descriptive feedback that addresses not only the quality of the current work but how to improve or move to the next step in learning should be provided to each student. Schools also help families see how a student's performance corresponds with national or state norms.

> Assessment should emphasize individual progress rather than comparison with other students and not rely on extrinsic motivation.

An important part of student self-assessment is reflecting on personal growth and learning, communicating what they have learned, and identifying further learning goals. Student-led conferences are especially valuable in achieving the goals of an assessment and reporting program. Various written reports from students and teachers, telephone calls, and e-mail messages keep home and school working together. Major learning activities or units should culminate in some form of presentation or product that students share with their parents, other students, or the community to demonstrate what they have learned and accomplished.

Leadership and Organization Characteristics

A shared vision developed by all stakeholders guides every decision. (Shared Vision)

Vision has been viewed as an acute sense of the possible. Research and exemplary practice over the past four decades have provided middle level educators with a strong sense of what is, indeed, possible in the education of young adolescents. Idealistic and uplifting, the resulting vision reflects our best knowledge and lights the way toward achieving a truly successful middle level school for every young adolescent. It reveals how research and practice can work in harmony to create a school in which every student experiences success. While a school leader has a personal vision of what the school can become, it is important to build the school's vision collaboratively around a set of core beliefs that are understood, owned, and supported by the larger school community.

The vision becomes the basis for a concise, collaboratively developed mission statement supported by all stakeholders—students, teachers, administrators, families, board of education members, and the community. School leaders regularly ask for input into the vision and mission statements from students, parents, and community so that both are seen as living foundational documents that guide all decisions made about the school.

The mission statement takes into account the district philosophy and goals as well as relevant official guidelines. The fundamental building blocks, however, must always include the learning each student needs to achieve, the very best knowledge we have about the human growth and development of youngsters ages 10 to 15, and the accepted principles of learning.

When a shared vision and mission statement become operational, middle grades educators implement appropriate practices to develop a challenging academic program; they develop criteria to guide decisions and a process to make needed changes. Periodically reviewing and possibly revising the vision and mission statements are important steps as circumstances change and new research and practices emerge.

Leaders are committed to and knowledgeable about this age group, educational research, and best practices. (Committed Leaders)

Effective leadership is the linchpin of a school's success. All those who serve as school leaders—whether administrators, teachers, or other staff members—must possess a deep understanding of the young adolescents with whom they work and the society in which they live. They must recognize their own strengths and capitalize on them. These leaders understand the complete spectrum of young adolescent development and use that knowledge to create middle grades programs that address the unique needs of these students and advance their learning and growth.

Effective principals consistently update their knowledge and understanding of research and best practices. Such leaders comprehend the nuances of teaming, student advocacy, and exploration, and possess a solid understanding of curriculum, pedagogy, and assessment practices. They use this information to empower others to make the often-needed, hard decisions as a school addresses the education and well-being of each and every student.

Middle grades leaders strive to educate colleagues, parents, policymakers, and community members about the middle school concept or philosophy, relevant research, and proven practices to build support for long-term, continuous school improvement. Although other stakeholders play important roles in developing successful schools for young adolescents, it is the middle school principal who has the central role, ensuring that policies and practices exist to make the school a learning place. As the prime determiner of the school culture and its direction, the principal influences student achievement and teacher effectiveness by using his or her knowledge to nurture, sustain, and advocate for a comprehensive, student-centered education program. An unwavering devotion to the growth and development of young adolescents characterizes an exemplary leader.

Leaders demonstrate courage and collaboration.
(Courageous & Collaborative Leaders)

As architects for change, effective leaders know that yesterday does not have to determine tomorrow. Courageous, collaborative leaders make a difference by putting their knowledge and beliefs into action. Their understanding and commitment to the successful education of every young adolescent help them challenge and change practices that do not serve students' best interests and confront those issues or situations that are out of alignment with the school's vision.

Successful principals use the expertise of a variety of people to ensure the academic growth and well-being of every student. Working together with a leadership team, the principal is responsible for building a culture of collaboration that values input from all members of the school community, cultivates leadership skills in others, and empowers them to make decisions and enact changes. The entire staff is involved in creating a learning community that places top priority on the education and healthy development of every student and adult within the community.

> Effective leaders challenge and change practices that do not serve students' best interests and confront issues not in line with the vision.

Principals and their leadership teams understand that schools committed to the long-term implementation of effective practices must be collaborative enterprises, for improvement cannot depend on any single person. They also recognize that improving schools is a long-term proposition. New structures, programs, and practices, to endure, must become integral to the school culture. Leaders inevitably serve as the ultimate role models. They know that the school itself is a teacher and that students learn not only from the instruction offered but from implicit lessons as well—the ways adults treat each other, set priorities, establish policies, and make decisions.

Ongoing professional development reflects best educational practices. (Professional Development)

Middle grades educators thrive on professional development. They recognize the positive impact it can have on teaching and learning when focused on improvements that directly relate to increased student academic growth and personal development. Too often, professional development programs have been a random set of activities with little or no direct relationship to known teacher, administrator, and school needs. Yet, a growing body of research and practice tells us effective professional development programs are those based on data collected about that school and the identified needs of teachers.

Properly focusing a school's professional development program calls for strong, collaborative leadership. It requires a school leader who facilitates and models learning, listens thoughtfully, and builds a school culture that supports faculty as they engage in reflective practice. Such a program is cognizant of the needs of adult learners, recognizing that like students, they have different learning styles and are at different places on the learning continuum. It is important that professional development experiences provide continued participation over an extended period, collaborative approaches, and ongoing assessment of the effectiveness of the professional development initiatives.

Such experiences can be offered in many forms including, but not limited to, structured sessions in which groups of teachers form learning communities to discuss shared professional readings, student data and work, and instructional and assessment strategies, or as multiple-phased workshops or programs focusing on specific school improvement practices or content knowledge. Professional development initiatives are enriched and extended through district, state, or national conferences, teacher mentors, workshops, university courses, and focused school visitations. Numerous Web-based opportunities facilitate differentiated learning and broaden professional networks while helping to eliminate the chronic time crunch as schools attempt to stay current with the latest research.

Organizational structures foster purposeful learning and meaningful relationships. (Organizational Structures)

The ways schools organize teachers and group and schedule students have a significant impact on the learning environment. The interdisciplinary team of two or more teachers working with a common group of students in a block of time is the signature component of high-performing schools, literally the heart of the school from which other desirable programs and experiences evolve. Although sometimes perceived primarily as an organizational arrangement, teaming must be much more. The team is the foundation for a strong learning community characterized by a sense of family. Students and teachers on the team become well acquainted, feel safe, respected, and supported, and are encouraged to take intellectual risks.

Effective interdisciplinary teams lead to improved student achievement, increased parental contacts, an enhanced school climate, and positive student attitudes.

Research indicates that effective interdisciplinary teams lead to improved student achievement, increased parental contacts, an enhanced school climate, and positive student attitudes. Experience has shown that smaller teams of two or three teachers are most effective in achieving these benefits. Furthermore, teaming has a positive impact on the professional lives of teachers, expanding a collegial focus. Whether organized formally or not, teachers of a particular subject must have regular opportunities to meet.

Daily or regular common planning time is essential so that teams can plan ways to integrate the curriculum, analyze assessment data, examine student work, discuss current research, and reflect on the effectiveness of instructional approaches being used. Addressing the concerns of individual students and day-to-day management details are important topics on a team's agenda but should be in balance with the essential work of considering curriculum, instruction, and assessment.

A schedule that provides large blocks of class time enables teaching teams to conduct valuable learning experiences such as field trips, debates, mock trials, community-based service activities, and science experiments not possible in the usual single period. In such a block schedule, a few students can be provided remedial support and others can be freed to do enrichment activities without interfering with the ongoing program. On occasion, two or three teams or an entire grade level can meet together during the block.

To counter the trend toward excessively large schools and achieve a desired sense of smallness, large schools are often subdivided into "houses" or "schools-within-a-school." These subdivisions replicate on a smaller scale the same mix of grade levels and ethnic and socioeconomic groups that make up the school as a whole. Such arrangements foster the long-term student-teacher relationships known to have real educational and developmental value during these transition years. Keeping a team of teachers and its students together for two or three years, as in looping and multiage teams, provides opportunities for teachers to establish sustained relationships with students and with parents and families.

> Keeping a team of teachers and students together for two or three years provides opportunities for teachers to establish sustained relationships with students and parents.

Research indicates the many limiting and negative effects of academic tracking—decreases in student motivation and self-esteem, unequal learning opportunities, and declines in the overall quality of education. In its place, successful middle grades schools use cooperative learning groups, independent study, enrichment programs, and other practices to respond to the variety of student competencies, interests, and abilities and meet the needs of advanced learners.

In exemplary middle level schools, teachers who work together on a team design and operate much of the program, collaborating across teaching specialties and sharing responsibility for literacy development, advocacy, and student life. They take advantage of opportunities to vary the use of time, space, staff, and grouping arrangements to achieve success for every student. Team leaders represent their teams on a school-wide leadership group that sets direction, provides feedback, and advances school improvement efforts.

Culture and Community Characteristics

The school environment is inviting, safe, inclusive, and supportive of all. (School Environment)

A successful school for young adolescents is an inviting, supportive, and safe place—a joyful community that promotes in-depth learning and enhances students' physical and emotional well-being. In such a school, human relationships are paramount.

The essence of a happy, healthy school is reflected in the talk one hears. Staff members are cordial to each other, teachers and administrators call students by name, and students interact comfortably and respectfully with adults and peers. Statements of encouragement and positive feedback substantially outnumber disciplinary or correctional comments. Interactions among staff members and between students reflect fairness and mutual respect. Teachers, staff, and students learn and put into practice the skills of direct feedback, mediation, healthy and appropriate confrontation, problem solving, positive risk taking, and personal and collaborative goal setting.

Everyone in an inviting school works proactively to eliminate harassment, verbal abuse, bullying, and name-calling. Students and teachers understand that they are part of a community in which differences are respected and celebrated. When an egalitarian concept is embedded in daily school life, less time is devoted to settling disputes and managing discipline. The safe and supportive environment encourages students to take intellectual risks, to be bold with their expectations, and to explore new challenges. Every student—no matter what creed, color, or uniqueness—is a genuine and contributing member of the school community.

Effective middle grades schools develop structures that ensure students will be known as individuals and feel cared for and valued. Instructional teams are essential to the process of creating learning communities. The team is a home away from home—the place where students work and learn together with teachers and classmates with whom they identify.

The school buildings and campus make an immediately visible statement about caring. An attractive, inviting, clean, and structurally sound physical plant is an expression of a supportive and safe environment. Student work is prominently displayed, an indication that learning is a school priority. Like the young adolescents themselves, the climate of a developmentally responsive middle level school requires constant nurturing.

Middle grades educators, students, and their families plan and implement effective transition programs in cooperation with the elementary school and with the high school. Such programs ensure all students entering a new school are successfully integrated into the school and are able to maintain their academic and social progress. These transition programs are ongoing processes that require multiple opportunities for students and their families to become familiar with and involved in various activities over time.

Every student's academic and personal development is guided by an adult advocate. (Adult Advocate)

Academic success and personal growth increase markedly when young adolescents' affective needs are met. Therefore, every adult in developmentally responsive middle level schools serves as an advocate, advisor, and mentor. The concept of advocacy is fundamental to the school's culture, embedded in its every aspect.

Advocacy is not a singular event or a period in the schedule, it is an attitude of caring that translates into actions, big and small, when adults respond to the needs of each young adolescent in their charge.

> Advocacy is an attitude of caring that translates into actions, big and small.

Young adolescents have many concerns about matters that lie outside the parameters of the academic curriculum, and they need opportunities to dialogue about these with one another and with a trusted adult. Each student must have one adult in the school who assumes special responsibility for supporting that student's academic and personal development. This adult is a model of good character who is knowledgeable about the development of young adolescents, enjoys working with them, and easily comes to know students well as individuals. Such advisors are not counselors, but they listen to and guide youth through the ups and downs of school life.

When students and their advisors meet regularly during the school day, an advisory program helps students develop respect for self and others; compassion; a workable set of values; and the skills of cooperation, decision making, and goal setting. The advisory program designed for the specific culture of the school and community meets the needs of that school's students. Advisors receive ongoing professional development to help them fulfill this vital role.

Serving as the primary liaison between the school and family, the advisor initiates contact with parents to provide pertinent information about the student's program and progress and receives calls from any family member with a concern. Helping families stay engaged in their children's education is a critical and difficult task. Students seeking independence often prefer to keep home and school separate, but active two-way communication leads to higher student achievement.

Advisors are in a position to recognize behavioral changes in students that should be brought to the attention of counselors, administrators, teachers, and parents. Advisors and all staff members should facilitate healthy and caring peer relationships by modeling the interpersonal relationships that define the school vision. Protecting young adolescents from bullying, for instance, begins when teachers in their classrooms and the total culture of the school promote compassion, understanding, and mutual respect.

> Successful middle grades schools provide continuity of caring and support that extends throughout the entire middle level experience.

To assist educators in fulfilling this advisory role, schools use a variety of organizational arrangements such as scheduled meetings of advisors and advisees, extended homerooms, and team-based mentorships. Such advisory efforts augment but do not replace comprehensive guidance and counseling services. Successful middle grades schools provide continuity of caring and support that extends not only throughout the day but throughout the entire middle level experience.

The importance of students' having adults who care about them is so essential that schools should look beyond school personnel for additional assistance. Volunteers from business partners, tutors, retired teachers, academic and athletic coaches, and personnel in after-school programs can connect with students and also serve as role models and advocates.

Comprehensive guidance and support services meet the needs of young adolescents. (Guidance Services)

Young adolescents are presented with innumerable and often fateful choices. Developmentally responsive middle grades schools, therefore, provide specialized professionals who are readily available to offer the assistance students may need in negotiating their lives both in and out of school. In effective middle grades schools, counselors, special needs teachers, school psychologists, social workers, school nurses, and community liaisons help young adolescents with learning difficulties, social adjustments, family issues, and health problems. They use their specific knowledge and skills to team with classroom teachers and administrators to promote students' academic progress. Consistent communication and interaction among specialists and classroom teachers help to assure student behaviors and learning needs are accurately assessed and met. All staff are aware of appropriate referral services and procedures when recommending students for specialized services.

School counselors support teachers in advisory programs, demonstrate and conduct classroom group activities, and offer both one-on-one and small-group guidance sessions for students as needed. They sponsor peer mediation and peer tutoring programs and share their expertise with teams and individual teachers, often serving as resource persons in classroom activities. They also meet with parents, usually in conjunction with teams or an individual teacher.

Parents need help in understanding the relationship between various middle grades course options and the high school's programs. School counselors facilitate the multidimensional transition programs for students entering and exiting the middle level school. An essential part of that transition is identifying the needs of every student and communicating an assistance plan to those responsible.

School counselors coordinate the support services provided by the school system to ensure the most effective use of specialists such as school psychologists, social workers, and speech therapists. They also see to it that guidance services are articulated with those of the district's elementary and high schools, and they access and coordinate community-based services for the well-being of students. As professionally prepared specialists, counselors should spend their time working directly with students and faculty rather than in administrative tasks.

Health and wellness are supported in curricula, school-wide programs, and related policies. (Health & Wellness)

Developmentally responsive middle level schools help students develop and maintain healthy minds and bodies and understand their own physical development. An emphasis on health, wellness, and safety permeates the entire school, with faculty members sharing responsibility for maintaining a healthy school environment. The risks associated with tobacco, alcohol, drugs, unhealthy eating habits, and sexual activities are addressed. Benefits and attributes of healthy lifestyles are supported through curriculum programs and the learning environment as a whole.

A coordinated health program concentrates on those areas of students' personal lives that either enhance or interfere with learning. These areas provide opportunities for developing and practicing healthful decision-making and refusal skills, which are purposely reinforced throughout the curriculum. Written policies support and direct a school's efforts to address health and wellness within courses, the school culture, school and community collaborative projects, and parent partnerships. All adults are encouraged to model good health habits. Local health agencies cooperate with the school and families in dealing with young adolescent health issues. Schools actively promote a safe and welcoming environment by developing school and community-wide initiatives that identify risks and promote protective conditions through a true home-school community partnership.

A comprehensive health and wellness program includes student-focused, integrated experiences that are implemented throughout the curriculum, plus regular physical education activities that improve students' cardiovascular fitness, coordination, agility, and strength. The school emphasizes lifelong physical activities such as aerobics, dance, leisure-time sports, and fitness programs. Intramural and co-curricular activities that require physical activity must be developmentally appropriate, open to the entire student body, and comply with recognized national standards. Schools that engage in interscholastic sports follow policies and practices that are developmentally responsive. Schools also recognize students for gains they make toward fulfilling personal goals through individual wellness profiles.

> A coordinated health program concentrates on those areas of students' lives that either enhance or interfere with learning.

A school that fosters physical and psychological safety strives to build resiliency in young people by maintaining an environment in which peaceful and safe interactions are expected and supported by written policies, scheduled professional development, and student-focused activities. These policies are communicated to students, teachers, and families. A strong sense of school community is developed by helping students learn how to manage anger, resolve conflicts peacefully, and prevent hateful or violent behaviors such as bullying.

Schools with policies, professional development plans, and both formal and informal curricula that consistently address the issues previously mentioned will also succeed in fostering health and wellness. In such schools every student has an increased sense of well-being, which, in turn, increases the likelihood of his or her academic success.

The school actively involves families in the education of their children. (Family Involvement)

More than ever, schools and families must work together to provide the best possible learning experiences for every young adolescent. Too many parents become less involved in the middle grades school than they were in elementary school, believing that their children need less support at this level. Continuing parental involvement is as important as ever, so schools must create a family-friendly environment and take the initiative in forging needed home-teacher-school bonds. Frequently, parents are uncertain about how they can be involved in this new, and often larger, school and may also be unsure about the most appropriate way to deal with their rapidly changing and maturing child but are hesitant to seek assistance.

Research studies clearly link the involvement of both family and other adults in the community with higher levels of student achievement, improved student behavior, and greater overall support for schools. Standards promoting home-school partnerships are essential and should be used in every school. Such standards generally call for regular, two-way communication between home and school; promotion and support of parenting skills; active parent participation in student learning through a variety of activities and roles; and parents involved in decision making at schools. Successful middle level schools, therefore, promote family involvement by sponsoring parent education programs, creating and maintaining links between home and school, initiating volunteer programs, and establishing coordinated home-school learning experiences.

> Research studies clearly link the involvement of family and other adults in the community with higher levels of student achievement.

Administrators and faculty members in these schools use a variety of ways to reach out to families to solicit input: holding meetings in community centers; using language interpreters; or setting up a school family learning center, where parents can obtain information, have materials translated, or meet with school officials and other parents. The traditional and still important practices of school newsletters, report cards, and parent-teacher conferences have been joined and enhanced by e-mail, websites, student-led conferences, and homework hotlines as valuable communication tools to inform and involve parents and community members.

Ultimately, the school staff must work aggressively to make families feel welcome in the school—and partner with them in the education and development of their shared young people. Schools should communicate an expectation that families will take advantage of opportunities provided to support student learning. Further, families should be encouraged to spend time engaged in their children's learning, thus demonstrating their belief in the importance of school success. When collaborating with families, educators must be sensitive to local and cultural considerations and to the various types of family structures.

The school includes community and business partners.

(Community & Business)

Schools do not presume to educate children alone. In today's society, genuine community involvement is a fundamental component of successful schools for young adolescents. Therefore, middle level schools seek appropriate partnerships with businesses, social service agencies, and organizations with purposes consistent with the school's mission.

The community is an excellent resource, serving as a site for learning experiences that cannot be provided in a classroom, as a source of materials and guest experts, and providing assistance in appropriate learning initiatives for students and faculty. Students can become involved in apprenticeships, shadow studies, service-learning projects, and after-school programs that use the community as a learning site. Likewise, business partners can permit employees to share their expertise in the school's instructional program, grant time off for parents to attend student-teacher-parent conferences and school events, and provide assistance in school programs that recognize students' accomplishments and offer learning initiatives.

In any partnership or venture, all parties must benefit and share mutually understood roles and expectations. The school-business relationship is no different. Written guidelines for business partnerships should be developed to ensure consistent and mutually beneficial agreements are reached while keeping what is best for young adolescents the focus of every agreement. When collaborating with business partners, educators must be sensitive to corporate, local, and cultural considerations, while business partners must be sensitive to the needs of young adolescent learners and the mission of the school.

Call to Action

The importance of middle level education can never be overestimated. The future of individuals and, indeed, that of society is largely determined by the nature of the educational experiences of young adolescents during these formative years. Creating and maintaining schools that fulfill the broad responsibilities of middle level education require extensive support. Such support from the profession as well as the general population must evolve from a full understanding of young adolescents and the types of programs and practices known to be effective for them. In *This We Believe: Keys to Educating Young Adolescents,* we have provided the ideas and ideals necessary to establish such programs, wherever they may be housed.

AMLE's advocacy is representative of long-standing and research-supported beliefs about effective education that are applicable for all grades. Its central tenets are found in current reform initiatives for high schools and elementary schools. These and other initiatives draw from the same progressive foundations on which middle level education is based.

All stakeholders must recognize that middle level education serves a distinct developmental period, one in which youth undergo major changes in every aspect of their being. Because young adolescents move through the many maturation and development stages as individuals at such widely varying times and rates, and because the values, attitudes, interests, and habits of mind they formulate have lifelong implications, providing an appropriate education program for this age group is an especially challenging, yet critically important task. As the limitations of high-stakes-testing-only reform become apparent, there is a readiness for instituting more philosophically sound and research-supported improvements—in short, the middle school concept as delineated in this document.

Our call to action requires a recommitment to the philosophy of middle level education by some and a newfound commitment by others. The vision described in *This We Believe: Keys to Educating Young Adolescents* advocates for what research shows is right for young adolescents, not what might be current practice, expedient, or readily accomplished. Thoroughly preparing all young adolescents to succeed in a demanding and evolving global culture makes the transformation and improvement of middle level education an imperative. We ask you to join in this vital effort by

» Becoming personally familiar with the contents of this position statement, studying it sufficiently so that you have a clear understanding of its advocacy and can articulate it to others.

» Engaging one or two colleagues in discussion about this position paper, sharing views, clarifying thinking, and considering the implications of putting it more fully into practice.

» Exploring with faculty and administrators specific ways to use *This We Believe: Keys to Educating Young Adolescents* as an integral part of your school's collaborative professional development opportunities.

» Assessing the degree to which your school currently implements the 16 characteristics of a developmentally responsive school.

» Developing a focused school improvement plan aimed at full implementation of the recommended characteristics.

» Engaging pertinent stakeholders—boards of education, district office personnel, and parents—in learning experiences that will increase their knowledge and understanding of the academic and developmental needs of middle grades students.

If all of us take these critical steps, we will achieve developmentally responsive, challenging, exploratory, and equitable middle grades schools in which all students can excel.

Research Supporting
This We Believe

〰〰〰〰〰〰〰〰〰〰〰〰〰〰〰〰〰〰〰〰〰〰〰〰〰〰〰〰〰〰〰

The research base that supports the middle school concept and middle level education continues to grow. In *Research and Resources in Support of This We Believe* (Caskey, Andrews, Bishop, Capraro, Roe, & Weiss, 2010), a companion volume to *This We Believe: Keys to Educating Young Adolescents,* the AMLE Research Advisory Committee summarized the salient research. Numerous other studies appear in issues of *Research in Middle Level Education Online, Middle Grades Research Journal,* and other peer-reviewed journals as well as compendiums such as *The Handbook of Research in Middle Level Education* series and the *Middle Level Education Research Annual.* In addition, recent reports have highlighted the critical importance of the middle grades for keeping students on track for high school graduation (Balfanz, Herzog, & Mac Iver, 2007; Balfanz, 2009) and beyond (ACT, 2008). This expanding research base warrants attention by middle grades practitioners and educational policymakers when considering programs and practices for young adolescents.

In this section, we provide a brief summary of the major research findings in the three categories of characteristics that frame this new edition of *This We Believe* followed by specific, recent examples of studies that support those findings.

References:

ACT. (2008). *The forgotten middle: Ensuring that all students are on target for college and career readiness before high school.* Iowa City, IA: Author.

Balfanz, R. (2009). *Putting middle grades students on the graduation path: A policy and practice brief.* Westerville, OH: National Middle School Association.

Balfanz, R., Herzog, L., & Mac Iver, D. (2007). Preventing student disengagement and keeping students on the graduation path in urban middle grade schools: Early identification and effective interventions. *Educational Psychologist, 42*(4), 223–235.

Caskey, M. M., Andrews, P.G., Bishop, P.A., Capraro, R. M., Roe, M., & Weiss, C. (2010). *Research and resources in support of This We Believe.* Westerville, OH: National Middle School Association.

Curriculum, Instruction, and Assessment

Research on effective *Curriculum, Instruction, and Assessment* for young adolescents reveals that teaching and learning strategies employed in middle grades classrooms should be as diverse, varied, and lively as the students themselves. The integrative curriculum design promises much for middle grades teachers who wish to develop classroom curriculum that encourages young adolescents to actively engage in their learning. The varied learning and teaching approaches in effective middle grades classrooms are often characterized by an inquiry-oriented, problem-based framework that calls for interdisciplinary, student-centered lessons grounded in real-world issues. Engaging students in meaningful learning experiences such as these requires educators who understand early adolescence and who have been specifically prepared to teach in the middle grades.

Nesin, G. (2005). Students and teachers engaged in active learning. In T. Erb (Ed.), *This we believe in action: Implementing successful middle level schools* (pp. 53–62).Westerville, OH: National Middle School Association.

> Citing reports from the National Research Council and other researchers, Nesin noted that a safe and supportive classroom community must be in place for active learning to occur and that students and teachers hold joint responsibility for their interactions and learning. Nesin included a set of implications for practice and examples that contrast passive and active learning.

Gutstein, E. (2003). Teaching and learning mathematics for social justice in an urban, Latino school. *Journal for Research in Mathematics Education, 34,* 37–73.

> Using the National Council of Teachers of Mathematics standards-based curriculum, Gutstein described the role of teaching and learning mathematics in an urban, Latino classroom. Gutstein also delineated a series of real-world projects that changed students' attitudes toward mathematics.

Dowden, T. (2007). Relevant, challenging, integrative, and exploratory curriculum design: Perspectives from theory and practice for middle level schooling in Australia. *The Australian Educational Researcher, 34*(2), 51–72.

Dowden examined theories supporting integrative and multidisciplinary models of curriculum integration with respect to middle level curriculum reform and traced a century of development of curriculum integration in the U.S.

Black, P., Harrison, C., Lee, C., Marshall, B., & Wiliam, D. (2004). Working inside the black box: Assessment for learning in the classroom. *Phi Delta Kappan, 86*(1), 9–21.

Building on their seminal research report, "Inside the Black Box: Raising Standards Through Classroom Assessment," Black and colleagues conducted a follow-up study in secondary schools. They explored how teachers changed their practice and students changed their behavior to improve student learning. They described the effects of specific actions (i.e., questioning, feedback through grading, peer- and self-assessment, formative use of summative tests) and noted that teachers and students share responsibility for students' learning.

Mertens, S. B., Flowers, N., & Mulhall, P. (2002). The relationship between middle-grades teacher certification and teaching practices. In V. A. Anfara, Jr., & S. L. Stacki (Eds.), *Middle school curriculum, instruction, and assessment* (pp. 119–138). Greenwich, CT: Information Age Publishing.

Through analysis of survey data from more than 2,000 teachers in 134 schools (Michigan Middle Start Initiative), researchers concluded that middle grades and elementary-certified teachers were more likely to engage in effective classroom practices. Furthermore, in schools where teaming and high levels of common planning time were the norm, middle grades-certified faculty reported the highest levels of effective team and classroom practices.

Leadership and Organization

Research on effective *Leadership and Organization* comprises three broad categories: (1) professional development for teachers, (2) professional learning communities among teachers, and (3) the role of the instructional leader. The intersection of these dynamic and vital areas revolves around the principal's ability to provide vision, model innovations, offer individualized support to teachers, foster open and effective communication, and to function as an instructional resource. Instructional leaders can precipitate professional development that creates consistent and unified learning opportunities for teachers. Finally, when instructional leaders provide teachers with opportunities to build professional learning communities using common planning time and teaming, teachers become more satisfied with their jobs and students improve academically.

Garet, M. S., Porter, A. C., Desimone, L., Birman, B. F., & Yoon, K. S. (2001). What makes professional development effective? Results from a national sample of teachers. *American Educational Research Journal, 38*(4), 915–945.

> This large-scale research study compared the effects of different professional development components on teacher learning. Features that had a positive effect on teacher knowledge, skills, and classroom practice include those that (a) focus on content knowledge, (b) provide opportunities for active learning, and (c) are consistent with other learning activities.

Flowers, N., Mertens, S., & Mulhall, P. (1999). The impact of teaming: Five research-based outcomes of teaming. *Middle School Journal, 31*(2), 57–60.

> This research indicated the positive effect of interdisciplinary teaming and revealed (a) the critical nature of common planning time, (b) teaming improves school climate, (c) teaming increases parent communication, (d) teaming increases teachers' job satisfaction, and (e) teaming positively influences student achievement.

Marks, H. M., & Printy, S. M. (2003). Principal leadership and school performance: An integration of transformational and instructional leadership. *Educational Administration Quarterly, 39*(3), 370–397.

> This research study examined teacher-principal collaboration and its effect on teaching and student achievement. Results indicated that transformational and shared instructional leadership lead to a positive effect on the quality of teaching and student performance.

Valentine, J., Clark, D., Hackmann, D., & Petzko, V. (2004). *A national study of leadership in middle level schools: Volume II: Leadership for highly successful middle level schools.* Reston, VA: National Association of Secondary School Principals.

> This national research study examined middle level leadership of highly successful principals and their schools. The results revealed that critical leadership behaviors include (a) providing vision, (b) modeling behavior, (c) cultivating commitment, (d) providing individualized support for teachers, (e) communicating effectively, (f) being a resource provider, and (g) serving as an instructional resource.

Culture and Community

Research on effective *Culture and Community* demonstrates the importance of parent involvement, students' sense of belonging, peer relationships, and community context in maximizing achievement. While a teacher's responsibility for student achievement goes uncontested, a range of influences within and outside the classroom setting matter. An attention to culture and community underscores the range of influences and practices that warrant attention.

Mo, Y., & Singh, K. (2008). Parents' relationships and involvement: Effects on students' engagement and performance. *RMLE Online, 31*(10). Available at http://www.amle.org/Publications/RMLEOnline/Articles/Vol31No10/tabid/1696/Default.aspx

> Mo and Singh unveiled significant effects of parents' relationships and involvement on students' academic success.

Morocco, C. C., Clark-Chiarelli, N., Aguilar, C. M., & Brigham, N. (2002). Cultures of excellence and belonging in urban middle schools. *RMLE Online, 25*(2), 1–15. Available at http://www.amle.org/Publications/RMLEOnline/Articles/Vol25No2Article4/tabid/512/Default.aspx

> Based on a qualitative investigation across a three-year period, these researchers established the importance of features that define a high-performing culture that accommodates a range of students: (a) a philosophical system that believes in all students' achievement, commits to a collaborative learning environment, and supports students' development as lifelong learners; (b) administrators and school leaders who can respond to challenging situations when they arise; (c) collaborative organizational structures such as teaming and grouping; (d) coherent and consistent instructional practices that students experience across classrooms; (e) articulated understandings of the definition of a learner; (f) a consistent discourse about student learning; and (g) partnerships between and among parents, community, and school personnel.

Nelson, R. M., & DeBacker, T. K. (2008). Achievement motivation in adolescents: The role of peer climate and best friends. *Journal of Experimental Education, 76*(2), 170–189.

> Based on a self-report questionnaire, the researchers determined the variance in achievement motivation explained by peer relationships. Specifically, adolescents who felt valued and respected by their peers reported higher levels of achievement motivation.

Cook, T. D., Herman, M. R., Phillips, M., & Settersten, R.A. (2002). Some ways in which neighborhoods, nuclear families, friendship groups, and schools jointly affect changes in early adolescent development. *Child Development, 73*(4), 1283–1309

> In this examination of the many contextual influences on adolescents' lives, the authors find that students perform better in school when schools hold students to high academic standards, have an efficient organization with well-trained teachers, and are supported by involved parents.

Research Advisory Board authors:

Micki M. Caskey, P. Gayle Andrews, Penny A. Bishop, Robert M. Capraro, Mary Roe, and Christopher Weiss.

Characteristics of Young Adolescents

~~~
◇◇◇◇◇◇◇◇◇◇◇◇◇◇◇◇◇◇◇◇◇◇◇◇◇◇◇◇◇◇◇◇◇◇◇◇◇◇◇◇◇◇◇◇◇◇◇◇
~~~

This special section on the characteristics of young adolescents was prepared by Dr. Peter C. Scales, senior fellow, Office of the President, Search Institute. Dr. Scales, a developmental psychologist, author, speaker, and researcher, is widely recognized as one of the nation's foremost authorities on adolescent development. His recent studies have focused on identifying and promoting "developmental assets," those conditions that are linked to young people's success in school and in life. Middle grades educators are in a unique position to help build these developmental assets such as feeling empowered, playing useful roles, building social competence, and developing a commitment to learning, all of which are goals of middle level education.

~~~
◇◇◇◇◇◇◇◇◇◇◇◇◇◇◇◇◇◇◇◇◇◇◇◇◇◇◇◇◇◇◇◇◇◇◇◇◇◇◇◇◇◇◇◇◇◇◇◇
~~~

Youth between the ages of 10 and 15 are characterized by their diversity as they move through the pubertal growth cycle at varying times and rates. Yet, as a group, they reflect important developmental characteristics that have major implications for parents, educators, and others who care for them and seek to promote their healthy growth and positive development.

The following are what research suggests are notable characteristics of young adolescents in the physical, cognitive, moral, psychological, and social-emotional dimensions of development, with some points accenting their spiritual development. Although most young adolescents will exhibit these characteristics to some degree, the relative importance of each characteristic can vary widely depending on the individual. Gender, race, ethnicity, and other cultural influences, family and economic situations, learning and physical disabilities, a young adolescent's temperament, and qualities of his or her community or neighborhood are just some of the factors that, working together, give these developmental dimensions and characteristics their personal and social meaning.

These characteristics also are presented in sequential fashion, but of course, they are not experienced in that way. Rather, all the dimensions are intertwined, each affecting and being affected by the others. For example, how young adolescents develop physically has ramifications for how they think of themselves psychologically, and for how they interact socially with others. Because of many interconnections, the categories to which these developmental characteristics are assigned—psychological development rather than social-emotional, or cognitive rather than moral—are relatively arbitrary.

Young adolescents have a greater influence on their own developmental paths than they did in middle childhood. Most, if not all, of the characteristics highlighted here are the result of a give and take between the young adolescent and his or her environment. These recurring interactions produce an infinite variety of developmental nuances that combine to reflect each young adolescent's unique personhood. *Consequently, each of the characteristics listed here should be understood as a reasonable generalization for most young adolescents, one that is more or less valid for particular young adolescents in particular situations.* This is especially true for young adolescents in differing cultural contexts. Variations in race, ethnicity, socioeconomic status, sexual orientation, immigration history and language usage, and physical and mental abilities, among other factors, can influence how young adolescents experience their development, and the resulting implications for educators.

In this section, we occasionally note specific examples of cultural variation in these developmental characteristics. All of these examples have been empirically well established in the research literature. These examples are meant to illustrate the level of depth and concreteness with which middle grades educators should be familiar with *average* group cultural variation. The examples are not intended to reinforce old or create new stereotypes. A young adolescent might be "in" a given group, but that does not mean he or she will show a given variation, any more than not being in that cultural group means a given young adolescent will not show that variation. For example, it is well established that students living in poverty, as a group, are well behind socioeconomically more advantaged students in reading levels, but some students living in poverty are excellent readers, and some students from affluent backgrounds struggle with reading. The examples are intended only to remind middle grades educators that the cultural context in which young people develop has important implications for student engagement and learning. Therefore, knowledge of and sensitivity to specific intersections of cultural background and learning is a key priority for ongoing middle grades educator professional development.

In the area of physical development, young adolescents

» Experience rapid, irregular physical growth.

» Undergo bodily changes that may cause awkward, uncoordinated movements.

» Have varying maturity rates, with girls tending to begin puberty one and one-half to two years earlier than boys, and young adolescents in some cultural groups tending to begin puberty earlier than those in other groups (African-American youth, for example, begin puberty earlier than European-American youth, on average).

» Experience restlessness and fatigue due to hormonal changes.

» Need daily physical activity because of increased energy, and if not actively engaged in regular physical activity, often lack fitness, with poor levels of endurance, strength, and flexibility.

» Need to release energy, often resulting in sudden, apparently meaningless outbursts of activity.

» Have preferences for junk food but need good nutrition.

» May be prone to risky dieting practices in order to lose or gain weight (a practice found especially prevalent among European-American youth).

» Continue to develop sexual awareness, which increases with the onset of menstruation, the growth spurt, and the appearance of secondary sex characteristics.

» Are concerned with bodily changes that accompany sexual maturation and changes resulting in an increase in nose size, protruding ears, long arms, and awkward posture, concerns magnified because of comparison with peers.

» Have an increased need for comprehensive, medically accurate education about sexuality and health issues that responds to these increased concerns.

» Are physically vulnerable because they may adopt poor health habits or engage in experimentation with alcohol and other drugs and high-risk sexual behaviors.

In the area of cognitive-intellectual development, young adolescents

» Display a wide range of individual intellectual development.

» Increasingly are able to think abstractly, not only concretely; both concrete and abstract thinking styles may be in evidence in the same young adolescent, depending on the issue or situation.

» Commonly face decisions that require more sophisticated cognitive and social-emotional skills.

» Are intensely curious and have a wide range of intellectual pursuits, although few are, or need to be, sustained.

» Prefer active over passive learning experiences; depending on their cultural backgrounds, some young adolescents may be quite engaged in learning through observation but might not always show this engagement through the active participation that is typically desired and rewarded by teachers (these learning and participation strategies have been noted as more common among Native American students, for example).

» Prefer interaction with peers during learning activities.

» May show disinterest in conventional academic subjects, but are intellectually curious about the world and themselves.

» Respond positively to opportunities to connect what they are learning to participation in real-life situations such as community service projects. Research has shown such experiences may be particularly valuable in helping students from lower-income backgrounds become more engaged with school.

» Develop an increasingly more accurate understanding of their current personal abilities, but may prematurely close doors to future exploration in particular interest areas due to feeling inadequate in comparison to peers.

» Are developing a capacity to understand higher levels of humor, some of which may be misunderstood by adults to be overly sarcastic or even aggressive.

» Are inquisitive about adults and are keen observers of them; depending on their cultural upbringing, some young adolescents also may often challenge adults' authority.

In the area of moral development, young adolescents

» Are in transition from moral reasoning that focuses on "what's in it for me" to consideration of the feelings and rights of others; self-centered moral reasoning may be in evidence at the same time as principle-oriented reasoning, depending on the situation; in addition, cultural differences in the socialization of moral development, especially among young adolescents whose families are recent immigrants, may contribute to special moral conflicts or dilemmas for those young people attempting to navigate multiple cultures.

» Increasingly are capable of assessing moral matters in shades of grey as opposed to viewing them in black and white terms more characteristic of younger children; however, this increased potential for more complex moral reasoning may often not be evident in practice.

» Are generally idealistic, desiring to make the world a better place and to make a meaningful contribution to a cause or issue larger than themselves.

» Often show compassion for those who are downtrodden or suffering and have special concern for animals and the environmental problems that our world faces.

» Are capable of and value direct experience in participatory democracy.

» Owing to their lack of experience, are often impatient with the pace of change, underestimating the difficulties in making desired social changes.

» Are likely to believe in and espouse values such as honesty, responsibility, and cultural acceptance, while at the same time learning that they and the people they admire also can be morally inconsistent, and can lie or cheat, avoid responsibility, and be intolerant.

» At times are quick to see flaws in others, but slow to acknowledge their own faults.

» Are often interested in exploring spiritual matters as part of growing their awareness of self and the world, the connections between self and others, and the development of a life of hope and purpose, even as they may become distant from formal religious organizations; for many youth, however, connections to religious organizations may continue to be a vital part of early adolescence, such as among African American youth for whom religious connections have been found to be a particular source of strength.

» Are moving from acceptance of adult moral judgments to developing their own personal values; nevertheless, they tend to embrace major values consonant with those of their parents and other valued adults.

» Rely on parents and significant adults for advice, especially when facing major decisions.

» Greatly need and are influenced by trustworthy adult role models who will listen to them and affirm their moral consciousness and actions.

» Are increasingly aware of, concerned with, and vocal about inconsistencies between values exhibited by adults and the conditions they see in society.

In the area of psychological development, young adolescents

» Are often preoccupied with self, an intersection of psychological and spiritual development as they awaken to or become aware of their true essence or spirit.

» Seek to become increasingly independent, searching for adult identity and acceptance, but continue to need support and boundary-setting from adults; the search for independence may be stronger among youth who have been socialized in European-American cultures, whereas young adolescents from some cultural backgrounds such as Hispanic- or Asian-American youth, may be as or more focused on social obligations and roles in the family and other groups than they are on independence.

» May experience a significant increase in the awareness of and the importance they give to their ethnic identity.

» Experience levels of self-esteem that may fluctuate up and down, but in general are adequate and increase over time; in contrast, levels of belief in self-competence in academic subjects, sports, and creative activities often decline significantly from the levels of middle childhood.

» Typically get passionately and deeply involved with at least one talent, interest, or hobby that becomes a "spark" in their lives, giving them energy, joy, purpose, direction, and focus (but many need help identifying such sparks or passionate interests). Students from more economically disadvantaged backgrounds may be less able than more affluent students to identify and pursue their sparks unless schools maintain free or low-cost co-curricular programs that provide equity of access to these opportunities.

» Believe that personal problems, feelings, and experiences are unique to themselves.

» Tend to be self-conscious and highly sensitive to personal criticism.

» Desire recognition for their positive efforts and achievements.

» Exhibit intense concern about physical growth and maturity as profound physical changes occur.

» Increasingly behave in ways associated with their sex as traditional sex role identification strengthens for most young adolescents; some young adolescents may question their sexual identities.

» Are curious about sex, and have sexual feelings; they need to know that these are normal.

» Are psychologically vulnerable, because at no other stage in development are they more likely to encounter and be aware of so many differences between themselves and others.

» Are also psychologically resilient; across diversities in race and ethnicity, residence, or socioeconomic status, young adolescents tend to be optimistic and have a generally positive view of their personal future.

In the area of social-emotional development, young adolescents

» Have a strong need for approval and may be easily discouraged.

» Are increasingly concerned about peer acceptance.

» Often overreact to what many adults would consider relatively minor experiences of ridicule, embarrassment, and rejection.

» Although most young adolescents experience some of these discomforts as a typical part of growing up, other students can experience serious and harmful harassment, ridicule, and rejection (which decrease their feelings of safety at and engagement with school) due to their actual or perceived sexual orientation, religious background, immigrant or language status, or level of affluence.

» Are dependent on the beliefs and values of parents and other valued adults, but seek to make more of their own decisions.

» Increasingly welcome and benefit from positive relationships with adults outside their families, such as coaches, teachers, spiritual leaders, and neighbors, especially when these adults encourage, support, and nurture young adolescents' pursuit of their sparks or passionate interests.

» Enjoy fads, especially those shunned by adults.

» Have a strong need to belong to a group, with approval of peers becoming as important as adult approval, and on some matters even more important.

» Need moderate amounts of time alone to regroup and reflect on daily experiences.

» In their search for group membership, may experience significant embarrassment, ridicule, or rejection from those in other cliques from which they are excluded.

» Can gravitate toward affiliation with disruptive peers or membership in gangs in order to feel part of a group and to protect their physical safety.

» Experiment with new slang and behaviors as they search for a social position within their group, often discarding these "new identities" at a later date.

» Experience mood swings often with peaks of intensity and unpredictability.

» May exhibit immature behavior because their social skills and ability to regulate emotions frequently lag behind their cognitive and physical maturity. Among some young adolescents, however, particularly those whose cultural backgrounds value such capacities, their social and emotional skills may be more advanced than their cognitive and physical maturity suggest.

» Must adjust to the social acceptance of early maturing girls and boys, especially if they are maturing at a slower rate.

» If physically maturing earlier than peers, must deal with increased pressure around others' expectations of them, especially about engaging in high-risk behaviors.

» Often begin to experience feelings of sexual or romantic attraction to others, with some having significant sexual or romantic relationships, and a sizeable minority experiencing sexual behaviors.

» Often experience sexual harassment, bullying, and physical confrontations more than they did in elementary school or will in high school.

» Are often intimidated and frightened by their first middle grades experience because of the large numbers of students and teachers, the size of the building, and what may be for many their first day-to-day experiences with significant proportions of students who are culturally different from them.

» Are socially vulnerable, because, as they develop their beliefs, attitudes, and values, the emphasis media place on such things as money, fame, power, and beauty (and the majority culture perspectives that most often define those issues) may negatively influence their ideals and values, or encourage them to compromise their beliefs.

∞∞∞

For details on research studies supporting these characteristics and examples, see the numerous sources cited in Peter C. Scales and Nancy Leffert (2004), *Developmental Assets: A Synthesis of the Scientific Research on Adolescent Development* (2nd ed.), Minneapolis, MN: Search Institute, available from www.search-institute.org. In addition, see David Strahan, Mark L'Esperance, and John Van Hoose (2009), *Promoting Harmony: Young Adolescent Development and Classroom Practices* (3rd ed.), and Kenneth Brighton (2007), *Coming of Age: The Education and Development of Young Adolescents,* published by National Middle School Association and available at www.amle.org.

This We Believe:
A Historical Account

The history of middle level education spans a century. In the early days of the junior high school movement, 1910–1925, several widely recognized position statements set forth the goals and responsibilities of this fledgling American institution. Then in 1947 the six functions of the junior high school proposed by Gruhn and Douglass became the standard as efforts were made to revitalize the junior high. After the middle school was introduced in the 1960s, a number of materials about this new institution appeared.

In the midst of this emerging middle school movement, National Middle School Association (now AMLE) was started in 1973 by a group of college professors and middle level educators who saw a need for a national organization specifically focused on the education of young adolescents, ages 10 to 15. They convened annual conferences, published a few resources, and launched *Middle School Journal.* However, they realized no single comprehensive statement seemed to answer the frequently asked question, "Just what is a middle school?"

John Swaim, 1980 president of National Middle School Association, believed NMSA could make a significant contribution to middle level education by developing a clarifying document to answer this important question. He appointed a committee to prepare a position paper, which resulted in the 1982 publication of the original *This We Believe.*

While the first edition of *This We Believe* fulfilled the early need for professional guidelines, the AMLE Board of Trustees decided it should be a "living document." This meant it would periodically be reviewed, revised, and even re-conceptualized, if necessary, to ensure it continually represents what evolving research and practice tell us about educating young adolescents.

Since 1982, NMSA/AMLE has released three editions of *This We Believe*, each time honoring the commitment and vision of the original document. Many people have contributed to the development of these new editions, volunteering hours of time and professional expertise. To keep a historical record of their contributions, and in appreciation of their collective contributions to middle grades educators, we recognize the following people for their involvement in the various editions of *This We Believe*.

1980: *This We Believe*
Committee members: Alfred A. Arth, William Alexander, Charles Cherry, Donald Eichhorn, Conrad Toepfer, and Gordon Vars. Editor: John Lounsbury.

1995: *This We Believe: Developmentally Responsive Middle Level Schools*
Committee members: John Arnold, Sherrel Bergmann, Barbara Brodhagen, Ross Burkhardt, Maria Garza-Lubeck, John Lounsbury, Marion Payne, Chris Stevenson, Sue Swaim, and Gordon Vars. Writing Team: Ross Burkhardt, Gordon Vars, John Lounsbury, and Sue Swaim.

2003: *This We Believe: Successful Schools for Young Adolescents*
Committee members: Edward Brazee, Deborah Kasak, John Lounsbury, Gert Nesin, Charles Palmer, Linda Robinson, Sue Swaim, and Phyllis Toy Wong. Writing Team: Sue Swaim, John Lounsbury, and Edward Brazee.

A companion document, *Research and Resources in Support of This We Believe*, prepared by AMLE's Research Committee headed by Vincent A. Anfara, Jr., was released concurrently.

2010: *This We Believe: Keys to Educating Young Adolescents*
Committee members: Gayle Andrews, Jack Berckemeyer, Edward Brazee, Brenda Cassellius, Betty Edwards, Annette Fante, Bill Ferriter, Mark Springer, Sue Swaim, April Tibbles, Chris Toy, and Janet Vernon. Writing Team: Edward Brazee, John Lounsbury, Mark Springer, and Sue Swaim.

The Association for Middle Level Education

For more than 40 years, the Association for Middle Level Education (AMLE) has been a voice for those committed to the educational and developmental needs of students ages 10 to 15. AMLE helps middle grades educators reach every student, grow professionally, and create great schools. AMLE members are principals, teachers, school district personnel, professors, college students, parents, and community leaders across the United States and around the world. Our network of affiliate organizations in the United States, Canada, Europe, and Australia strengthens our outreach to the regional, state, provincial, and local levels.

AMLE provides professional development, periodicals, books, research, and other valuable information to assist educators on an ongoing basis. Our annual conference and leadership institutes offer the largest and most comprehensive professional learning opportunities for middle grades educators.

If you are interested in the education and well-being of students in the middle grades, we welcome you to join us.

Web — www.amle.org
Twitter — @AMLE
Facebook — facebook.com/amle.org